Singapore
MATH

MENTAL MATH

Strategies and Process Skills to Develop Mental Calculation

Grade 3
(Level 2)

Frank Schaffer

An imprint of Carson-Dellosa Publishing LLC

Greensboro, North Carolina

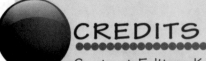

CREDITS

Content Editor: Karen Cermak-Serfass
Copy Editor: Barrie Hoople
Layout Design: Van Harris

This book has been correlated to state, common core state, national, and Canadian provincial standards. Visit www.carsondellosa.com to search for and view its correlations to your standards.

Copyright © 2011, Singapore Asian Publications (S) Pte Ltd

Frank Schaffer
An imprint of Carson-Dellosa Publishing LLC
PO Box 35665
Greensboro, NC 27425 USA

ISBN 978-1-936024-09-4

05-265141151

ABOUT THIS BOOK

Welcome to Singapore Math! The national math curriculum used in Singapore has been recognized worldwide for its excellence in producing students highly skilled in mathematics. The country's students have ranked at the top in achievement in the world on the Trends in International Mathematics and Science Study (TIMSS) in 1993, 1995, 2003, and 2008. The study also shows that students in Singapore are typically one grade level ahead of students in the United States. Because of these trends, Singapore Math has gained interest and popularity.

Mathematics in the Singapore primary (elementary) curriculum covers fewer topics but in greater depth. Key math concepts are introduced and built upon to reinforce various mathematical ideas and thinking. Singapore Math curriculum aims to help students develop the necessary math process skills for everyday life and to provide students with the opportunity to master math concepts.

Mental Math Level 2, for grade 3, provides a comprehensive guide for mastering mental calculation. Each strategy in this book helps students perform mental calculation and obtain accurate answers in the shortest possible amount of time.

This book consists of 52 practice and review pages. Each practice page demonstrates a strategy with an example and includes 10 problems for students to solve. Students can then test their understanding by working on the review pages that are located after the practice pages.

To help students build and strengthen their mental calculation skills, this book provides strategies that will benefit students as they learn tips to solve math problems quickly and effectively. After acquiring such invaluable skills, students can apply them to their future, real-life experiences with math, such as in shopping and banking. *Mental Math Level 2* is an indispensable resource for all students who wish to master mental strategies and excel in them.

TABLE OF CONTENTS

TABLE OF CONTENTS

STRATEGIES OVERVIEW

The following overview provides examples of the various math problem types and skill sets taught in Singapore Math.

1 Adding Three-Digit Numbers and Ones (Part 1)

562 + 7 = (500 + 60 + 2) + 7   ❑ Expand the three-digit number into hundreds, tens, and ones.

= (500 + 60) + (2 + 7)   ❑ Group the ones.

= 560 + 9   ❑ Add the numbers to find the answer.

= **569**

2 Adding Three-Digit Numbers and Ones (Part 2)

256 + 7 = (200 + 50) + (6 + 7)   ❑ Expand the numbers into hundreds, tens, and ones. Add the ones.

= 250 + 13   ❑ Expand the two-digit number. Add the tens values.

= (250 + 10) + 3

= 260 + 3   ❑ Add the numbers to find the answer.

= **263**

3 Adding Three-Digit Numbers and Ones (Part 3)

316 + 8 = 314 + 2 + 8   ❑ Break up the three-digit number to make a ten for easy addition.

= 314 + 10   ❑ Add the numbers to find the answer.

= **324**

4 Adding Three-Digit Numbers and 10

624 + 10 = **634**   ❑ Increase the value in the tens place by 1.

5 Adding Three-Digit Numbers and Two-Digit Numbers (Part 1)

762 + 29 = (760 + 2) + 29   ❑ Break up the three-digit number into a ten value and ones.

= 760 + (2 + 29)

= 760 + 31   ❑ Add the numbers to find the answer.

= **791**

7 Adding Three-Digit Numbers and Two-Digit Numbers (Part 2)

456 + 26 = 400 + 50 + 6 + 20 + 6   ❑ Expand the numbers into hundreds, tens, and ones.

= 400 + (50 + 20) + (6 + 6)   ❑ Arrange the numbers to add both the tens and ones values.

= 400 + 70 + 12

= 470 + 12   ❑ Add the numbers to find the answer.

= **482**

8 Adding Three-Digit Numbers and Two-Digit Numbers (Part 3)

236 + 49

49 ≈ 50   ❑ Round the two-digit number up to the nearest ten.

236 + 49 = 236 + (50 – 1)

= (236 + 50) – 1   ❑ Add the numbers.

= 286 – 1   ❑ Since 1 was added to 49 to make 50, subtract 1 from the sum to find the answer.

= **285**

9 Adding Three-Digit Numbers and 99

553 + 99 = 553 + 100 – 1   ❑ Add 1 to 99 to make 100.

= 653 – 1   ❑ Since 1 was added to 99, subtract 1 to find the answer.

= **652**

Helpful Hint: The hundreds place in the answer increases by 1 and the ones place in the answer decreases by 1.

10 Adding Three-Digit Numbers and Two-Digit Numbers Ending with 9

739 + 49 = (740 – 1) + (50 – 1)   ❑ Round each number up to the nearest ten.

= (740 + 50) – (1 + 1)   ❑ Arrange the numbers to add the tens and ones values.

= 790 – 2   ❑ Subtract 2 from the sum to find the answer.

= **788**

11 Adding Three-Digit Numbers and Tens

425 + 60 = **485**   ❑ Add the digits in the tens place.

13 Adding Three-Digit Numbers and 100

649 + 100 = **749**   ❑ Increase the value in the hundreds place by 1.

14 Adding Three-Digit Numbers and Three-Digit Numbers (Part 1)

367 + 173 = (367 + 3) + 170   ❑ Break up the second number for easy addition.

= 370 + 170

= (370 + 100) + 70   ❑ Break up and arrange the numbers for easy addition.

= 470 + 70

= (470 + 30) + 40   ❑ Break up the two-digit number for easy addition.

= 500 + 40

= **540**

15 Adding Three-Digit Numbers and Three-Digit Numbers (Part 2)

283 + 436

= (200 + 80 + 3) + (400 + 30 + 6)   ❑ Expand the numbers into hundreds, tens, and ones.

= (200 + 400) + (80 + 30) + (3 + 6)   ❑ Arrange the numbers to add the hundreds, tens, and ones values.

= 600 + 110 + 9   ❑ Add the numbers to find the answer.

= **719**

16 Adding Three-Digit Numbers and Three-Digit Numbers (Part 3)

186 + 395

395 ≈ 400   ❑ Round the second three-digit number up to the nearest hundred.

186 + 395 = 186 + (400 – 5)   ❑ Add the numbers.

= (186 + 400) – 5   ❑ Since 5 was added to 395 to make 400, subtract 5 from the sum to find the answer.

= 586 – 5

= **581**

17 Adding Three-Digit Numbers Ending with 9

309 + 499 = (310 – 1) + (500 – 1)   ❑ Round the numbers up to the nearest ten.

= (310 + 500) – (1 + 1)   ❑ Arrange the numbers to add the hundreds and ones values.

= 810 – 2   ❑ Subtract 2 from the sum to find the answer.

= **808**

19 Adding Three-Digit Numbers and Hundreds

487 + 300 = **787**   ❑ Add the digits in the hundreds place.

20 Subtracting Ones from Three-Digit Numbers (Part 1)

348 – 3 = (300 + 40 + 8) – 3   ❑ Expand the three-digit number into hundreds, tens, and ones.

= 340 + (8 – 3)   ❑ Subtract the ones.

= 340 + 5   ❑ Add the numbers to find the answer.

= **345**

21 Subtracting Ones from Three-Digit Numbers (Part 2)

242 – 5 = (232 + 10) – 5   ❑ Break up the three-digit number to make a ten for easy subtraction.

= 232 + (10 – 5)   ❑ Subtract from ten.

= 232 + 5   ❑ Add the numbers to find the answer.

= **237**

22 Subtracting Ones from Three-Digit Numbers (Part 3)

232 – 7 = 232 – (2 + 5)   ❑ Break up the one-digit number for easy subtraction.

= (232 – 2) – 5   ❑ Arrange the numbers for easy subtraction.

= 230 – 5   ❑ Subtract the numbers to find the answer.

= **225**

23 Subtracting 10 from Three-Digit Numbers

556 – 10 = **546** ❑ Decrease the value in the tens place by 1.

25 Subtracting Two-Digit Numbers from Three-Digit Numbers (Part 1)

445 – 32

= (400 + 40 + 5) – (30 + 2) ❑ Expand the numbers into hundreds, tens, and ones.

= (440 – 30) + (5 – 2) ❑ Arrange the numbers to subtract both the tens and ones values.

= 410 + 3 ❑ Add the numbers to find the answer.

= **413**

26 Subtracting Two-Digit Numbers from Three-Digit Numbers (Part 2)

472 – 35 = (432 + 40) – 35 ❑ Break up the three-digit number for easy subtraction.

= 432 + (40 – 35) ❑ Subtract the two-digit numbers.

= 432 + 5 ❑ Add the numbers to find the answer.

= **437**

27 Subtracting Two-Digit Numbers from Three-Digit Numbers (Part 3)

365 – 37 = 365 – (35 + 2) ❑ Break up the two-digit number for easy subtraction.

= (365 – 35) – 2 ❑ Subtract the two-digit number from the three-digit number.

= 330 – 2 ❑ Subtract the numbers to find the answer.

= **328**

28 Subtracting 99 from Three-Digit Numbers

551 – 99 = 551 – 100 + 1 ❑ Add 1 to 99 to make 100.

= 451 + 1 ❑ Since 1 was added to 99, add 1 to find the answer.

= **452**

Helpful Hint: The hundreds place in the answer decreases by 1 and the ones place in the answer increases by 1.

29 Subtracting Two-Digit Numbers Ending with 9 from Three-Digit Numbers

436 – 29

29 ≈ 30 ❑ Round the two-digit number up to the nearest ten.

436 – 29 = (436 – 30) + 1 ❑ Subtract the numbers.

= 406 + 1 ❑ Since 1 was added to 29 to make 30, add 1 to the difference to find the answer.

= **407**

31 Subtracting Tens from Three-Digit Numbers

684 – 50 = (604 + 80) – 50 ❑ Break up the three-digit number for easy subtraction.

= 604 + (80 – 50) ❑ Subtract the tens values.

= 604 + 30 ❑ Add the numbers to find the answer.

= **634**

32 Subtracting 100 from Three-Digit Numbers

843 – 100 = **743** ❑ Decrease the value in the hundreds place by 1.

33 Subtracting Three-Digit Numbers from Three-Digit Numbers (Part 1)

356 – 213

= (300 + 50 + 6) – (200 + 10 + 3) ❑ Expand the numbers into hundreds, tens, and ones.

= (300 – 200) + (50 – 10) + (6 – 3) ❑ Arrange the numbers to subtract the hundreds, tens, and ones values.

= 100 + 40 + 3 ❑ Add the numbers to find the answer.

= **143**

34 Subtracting Three-Digit Numbers from Three-Digit Numbers (Part 2)

610 – 435 = (110 + 500) – 435 ❑ Break up the first three-digit number for easy subtraction.

= 110 + (500 – 435) ❑ Subtract the numbers.

= 110 + 65 ❑ Add the numbers to find the answer.

= **175**

35 Subtracting Three-Digit Numbers from Three-Digit Numbers (Part 3)

985 – 437 = 985 – (435 + 2) ❑ Break up the second three-digit number for easy subtraction.

= (985 – 435) – 2 ❑ Subtract the three-digit numbers.

= 550 – 2 ❑ Subtract the numbers to find the answer.

= **548**

37 Subtracting Three-Digit Numbers Ending with 9 from Three-Digit Numbers

756 – 349

349 ≈ 350 ❑ Round the second three-digit number up to the nearest ten.

756 – 349 = (756 – 350) + 1 ❑ Subtract the numbers.

= 406 + 1 ❑ Since 1 was added to 349 to make 350, add 1 to the difference to find the answer.

= **407**

38 Subtracting Hundreds from Three-Digit Numbers

462 – 200 = **262** ❑ Subtract the hundreds values of both numbers.

39 Multiplication: Using Repeated Addition

3 × 4 = 4 + 4 + 4 ❑ When two numbers are multiplied, the answer can also be found with repeated addition. This problem shows 3 groups of 4.

= 8 + 4 ❑ Add the numbers to find the answer.

= **12**

Multiplication facts are widely used in mathematics. It is important to memorize the multiplication facts for 1 through 12.

40 Multiplying Numbers by 5

6 × 5 = **30** ❑ When even factors are multiplied by 5, the product will end in 0.

5 × 5 = **25** ❑ When odd factors are multiplied by 5, the product will end in 5.

Factors × 5	Product Begins With
2 and 3	1
4 and 5	2
6 and 7	3
8 and 9	4

41 Multiplying Numbers by 10

12 × 10 = **120** ❑ To multiply numbers by 10, put a 0 after the factor.

43 Dividing Numbers by 2, 3, and 4

To divide numbers by 2, 3, and 4, use what you know about fact families. Division and multiplication are inverse operations.

12 ÷ 2 = **6** ❑ The related fact is 6 × 2 = 12.

44 Dividing Numbers by 5 and 10

To divide numbers by 5, use what you know about the multiplication facts of 5.

20 ÷ 5 = **4** ❑ The related fact is 4 × 5 = 20.

To divide numbers by 10, remove the 0 from the divisor.

8Ø ÷ 1Ø = **8**

7

STRATEGY

Adding Three-Digit Numbers and Ones (Part 1)

Strategy

562 + 7 = (500 + 60 + 2) + 7   ❑ Expand the three-digit number into hundreds, tens, and ones.

        = (500 + 60) + (2 + 7)   ❑ Group the ones.

        = 560 + 9   ❑ Add the numbers to find the answer.

        = **569**

Solve each problem mentally.

1.   272 + 5 =

2.   190 + 3 =

3.   455 + 4 =

4.   761 + 7 =

5.   283 + 6 =

6.   830 + 9 =

7.   725 + 2 =

8.   321 + 8 =

9.   185 + 4 =

10.   863 + 3 =

Adding Three-Digit Numbers and Ones (Part 2)

Strategy

$256 + 7 = (200 + 50) + (6 + 7)$ ❑ Expand the numbers into hundreds, tens, and ones. Add the ones.

$\quad\quad = 250 + 13$ ❑ Expand the two-digit number. Add the

$\quad\quad = (250 + 10) + 3$ tens values.

$\quad\quad = 260 + 3$ ❑ Add the numbers to find the answer.

$\quad\quad = \mathbf{263}$

Solve each problem mentally.

1. $549 + 2 =$

2. $935 + 7 =$

3. $298 + 3 =$

4. $187 + 5 =$

5. $438 + 4 =$

6. $555 + 6 =$

7. $375 + 8 =$

8. $659 + 5 =$

9. $743 + 9 =$

10. $839 + 3 =$

Adding Three-Digit Numbers and Ones (Part 3)

Strategy

$316 + 8 = 314 + 2 + 8$

         $= 314 + 10$

         $= \mathbf{324}$

❑ Break up the three-digit number to make a ten for easy addition.
❑ Add the numbers to find the answer.

Solve each problem mentally.

1. $785 + 7 =$

2. $146 + 5 =$

3. $609 + 2 =$

4. $937 + 6 =$

5. $324 + 9 =$

6. $444 + 8 =$

7. $909 + 3 =$

8. $278 + 4 =$

9. $825 + 8 =$

10. $518 + 6 =$

Adding Three-Digit Numbers and 10

Strategy

624 + 10 = **634**

❏ Increase the value in the tens place by 1.

Solve each problem mentally.

1. 388 + 10 =

2. 970 + 10 =

3. 274 + 10 =

4. 685 + 10 =

5. 810 + 10 =

6. 426 + 10 =

7. 143 + 10 =

8. 758 + 10 =

9. 503 + 10 =

10. 847 + 10 =

WEEK 5 STRATEGY

Adding Three-Digit Numbers and Two-Digit Numbers (Part 1)

Strategy

762 + 29 = (760 + 2) + 29   ❑ Break up the three-digit number into a ten value and ones.

 = 760 + (2 + 29)

 = 760 + 31   ❑ Add the numbers to find the answer.

 = **791**

Solve each problem mentally.

1. 826 + 35 =

2. 165 + 16 =

3. 392 + 38 =

4. 528 + 45 =

5. 227 + 24 =

6. 466 + 17 =

7. 635 + 58 =

8. 732 + 40 =

9. 801 + 69 =

10. 374 + 29 =

GENERAL REVIEW 1

Solve each problem mentally.

1. 814 + 10 =

2. 617 + 9 =

3. 789 + 35 =

4. 731 + 8 =

5. 258 + 7 =

6. 106 + 10 =

7. 982 + 5 =

8. 450 + 6 =

9. 327 + 55 =

10. 546 + 8 =

STRATEGY

Adding Three-Digit Numbers and Two-Digit Numbers (Part 2)

Strategy

$456 + 26 = 400 + 50 + 6 + 20 + 6$

□ Expand the numbers into hundreds, tens, and ones.

$= 400 + (50 + 20) + (6 + 6)$

$= 400 + 70 + 12$

$= 470 + 12$

□ Arrange the numbers to add both the tens and ones values.

□ Add the numbers to find the answer.

$= \textbf{482}$

Solve each problem mentally.

1. $723 + 28 =$

2. $162 + 34 =$

3. $529 + 23 =$

4. $905 + 69 =$

5. $346 + 24 =$

6. $451 + 46 =$

7. $825 + 64 =$

8. $634 + 58 =$

9. $217 + 84 =$

10. $583 + 17 =$

Adding Three-Digit Numbers and Two-Digit Numbers (Part 3)

Strategy

236 + 49

49 ≈ 50

❏ Round the two-digit number up to the nearest ten.

236 + 49 = 236 + (50 − 1)

   = (236 + 50) − 1

   = 286 − 1   ❏ Add the numbers.

   = **285**   ❏ Since 1 was added to 49 to make 50, subtract 1 from the sum to find the answer.

Solve each problem mentally.

1. 547 + 39 =

2. 125 + 78 =

3. 628 + 47 =

4. 428 + 95 =

5. 235 + 27 =

6. 354 + 69 =

7. 874 + 88 =

8. 769 + 66 =

9. 907 + 19 =

10. 117 + 85 =

WEEK **9** STRATEGY

Adding Three-Digit Numbers and 99

Strategy

553 + 99 = 553 + 100 – 1   ❏ Add 1 to 99 to make 100.
       = 653 – 1   ❏ Since 1 was added to 99, subtract 1 to
       = **652**   find the answer.

Helpful Hint: The hundreds place in the answer increases by 1 and the ones place in the answer decreases by 1.

Solve each problem mentally.

1. 276 + 99 =

2. 652 + 99 =

3. 468 + 99 =

4. 813 + 99 =

5. 391 + 99 =

6. 548 + 99 =

7. 133 + 99 =

8. 866 + 99 =

9. 729 + 99 =

10. 387 + 99 =

STRATEGY

Adding Three-Digit Numbers and Two-Digit Numbers Ending with 9

Strategy

$739 + 49 = (740 - 1) + (50 - 1)$

$= (740 + 50) - (1 + 1)$

$= 790 - 2$

$= \textbf{788}$

❑ Round each number up to the nearest ten.
❑ Arrange the numbers to add the tens and ones values.
❑ Subtract 2 from the sum to find the answer.

Solve each problem mentally.

1. $219 + 49 =$

2. $899 + 29 =$

3. $479 + 69 =$

4. $719 + 59 =$

5. $159 + 19 =$

6. $689 + 49 =$

7. $829 + 79 =$

8. $569 + 59 =$

9. $309 + 89 =$

10. $639 + 39 =$

STRATEGY

Adding Three-Digit Numbers and Tens

Strategy

$425 + 60 = \mathbf{485}$ ❑ Add the digits in the tens place.

Solve each problem mentally.

1. $222 + 70 =$

2. $843 + 30 =$

3. $526 + 40 =$

4. $416 + 60 =$

5. $457 + 20 =$

6. $653 + 40 =$

7. $881 + 10 =$

8. $748 + 30 =$

9. $338 + 60 =$

10. $125 + 50 =$

GENERAL REVIEW 2

Solve each problem mentally.

1. $538 + 59 =$

2. $944 + 17 =$

3. $253 + 99 =$

4. $399 + 69 =$

5. $822 + 40 =$

6. $637 + 56 =$

7. $429 + 79 =$

8. $746 + 35 =$

9. $127 + 99 =$

10. $954 + 28 =$

STRATEGY

Adding Three-Digit Numbers and 100

Strategy

649 + 100 = **749**   ❑ Increase the value in the hundreds place by 1.

Solve each problem mentally.

1. 369 + 100 =

2. 636 + 100 =

3. 852 + 100 =

4. 175 + 100 =

5. 251 + 100 =

6. 652 + 100 =

7. 449 + 100 =

8. 548 + 100 =

9. 893 + 100 =

10. 717 + 100 =

Adding Three-Digit Numbers and Three-Digit Numbers (Part 1)

Strategy

$367 + 173 = (367 + 3) + 170$ ❑ Break up the second number for easy addition.
$= 370 + 170$
$= (370 + 100) + 70$ ❑ Break up and arrange the numbers for easy addition.
$= 470 + 70$
$= (470 + 30) + 40$ ❑ Break up the two-digit number for easy addition.
$= 500 + 40$
$= \textbf{540}$

Solve each problem mentally.

1. $236 + 224 =$

2. $623 + 217 =$

3. $418 + 322 =$

4. $856 + 114 =$

5. $107 + 543 =$

6. $521 + 139 =$

7. $375 + 555 =$

8. $733 + 117 =$

9. $468 + 372 =$

10. $776 + 174 =$

STRATEGY

Adding Three-Digit Numbers and Three-Digit Numbers (Part 2)

Strategy

283 + 436
= (200 + 80 + 3) + (400 + 30 + 6)   ❑ Expand the numbers into hundreds, tens, and ones.

= (200 + 400) + (80 + 30) + (3 + 6)   ❑ Arrange the numbers to add the hundreds, tens, and ones values.

= 600 + 110 + 9   ❑ Add the numbers to find the answer.
= **719**

Solve each problem mentally.

1. 326 + 103 =

2. 572 + 315 =

3. 671 + 226 =

4. 145 + 613 =

5. 817 + 130 =

6. 183 + 506 =

7. 456 + 323 =

8. 482 + 506 =

9. 206 + 511 =

10. 383 + 215 =

STRATEGY

Adding Three-Digit Numbers and Three-Digit Numbers (Part 3)

Strategy

186 + 395

$395 \approx 400$

186 + 395 = 186 + (400 − 5)
     = (186 + 400) − 5
     = 586 − 5

     = **581**

❏ Round the second three-digit number up to the nearest hundred.

❏ Add the numbers.
❏ Since 5 was added to 395 to make 400, subtract 5 from the sum to find the answer.

Solve each problem mentally.

1. 347 + 298 =

2. 493 + 399 =

3. 586 + 397 =

4. 118 + 599 =

5. 757 + 196 =

6. 179 + 598 =

7. 655 + 296 =

8. 484 + 499 =

9. 508 + 397 =

10. 238 + 496 =

WEEK 17 STRATEGY

Adding Three-Digit Numbers Ending with 9

Strategy

$309 + 499 = (310 - 1) + (500 - 1)$

$= (310 + 500) - (1 + 1)$

$= 810 - 2$

$= \mathbf{808}$

❑ Round the numbers up to the nearest ten.

❑ Arrange the numbers to add the hundreds and ones values.

❑ Subtract 2 from the sum to find the answer.

Solve each problem mentally.

1. $249 + 539 =$

2. $519 + 329 =$

3. $739 + 159 =$

4. $359 + 329 =$

5. $669 + 209 =$

6. $419 + 509 =$

7. $139 + 429 =$

8. $299 + 309 =$

9. $639 + 259 =$

10. $459 + 229 =$

GENERAL REVIEW 3

Solve each problem mentally.

1. 776 + 100 =

2. 284 + 136 =

3. 467 + 202 =

4. 392 + 568 =

5. 561 + 407 =

6. 625 + 163 =

7. 549 + 199 =

8. 279 + 459 =

9. 379 + 100 =

10. 878 + 102 =

WEEK 19

STRATEGY

Adding Three-Digit Numbers and Hundreds

Strategy

487 + 300 = **787**   ❑ Add the digits in the hundreds place.

Solve each problem mentally.

1. 593 + 200 =

2. 782 + 200 =

3. 355 + 500 =

4. 203 + 700 =

5. 675 + 100 =

6. 543 + 300 =

7. 891 + 100 =

8. 168 + 400 =

9. 647 + 200 =

10. 490 + 500 =

26

© Singapore Asian Publications (S) Pte Ltd

STRATEGY

Subtracting Ones from Three-Digit Numbers (Part 1)

Strategy

$348 - 3 = (300 + 40 + 8) - 3$ ❏ Expand the three-digit number into hundreds, tens, and ones.

$= 340 + (8 - 3)$ ❏ Subtract the ones.

$= 340 + 5$ ❏ Add the numbers to find the answer.

$= \mathbf{345}$

Solve each problem mentally.

1. $385 - 2 =$

2. $754 - 1 =$

3. $589 - 9 =$

4. $426 - 5 =$

5. $817 - 4 =$

6. $233 - 3 =$

7. $698 - 7 =$

8. $199 - 8 =$

9. $917 - 6 =$

10. $446 - 5 =$

Subtracting Ones from Three-Digit Numbers (Part 2)

Strategy

$242 - 5 = (232 + 10) - 5$ ❑ Break up the three-digit number to make a ten for easy subtraction.

$= 232 + (10 - 5)$ ❑ Subtract from ten.

$= 232 + 5$ ❑ Add the numbers to find the answer.

$= \textbf{237}$

Solve each problem mentally.

1. $273 - 7 =$

2. $734 - 5 =$

3. $936 - 9 =$

4. $162 - 8 =$

5. $383 - 6 =$

6. $407 - 9 =$

7. $565 - 8 =$

8. $611 - 4 =$

9. $834 - 6 =$

10. $371 - 2 =$

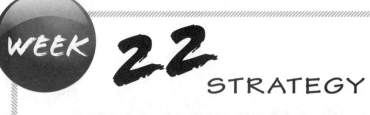

STRATEGY

Subtracting Ones from Three-Digit Numbers (Part 3)

Strategy

$232 - 7 = 232 - (2 + 5)$

$ = (232 - 2) - 5$

$ = 230 - 5$

$ = \mathbf{225}$

❑ Break up the one-digit number for easy subtraction.

❑ Arrange the numbers for easy subtraction.

❑ Subtract the numbers to find the answer.

Solve each problem mentally.

1. $324 - 8 =$

2. $652 - 4 =$

3. $193 - 6 =$

4. $293 - 5 =$

5. $761 - 9 =$

6. $596 - 7 =$

7. $413 - 8 =$

8. $814 - 5 =$

9. $365 - 8 =$

10. $715 - 9 =$

Subtracting 10 from Three-Digit Numbers

Strategy

556 − 10 = **546**   ❑ Decrease the value in the tens place by 1.

Solve each problem mentally.

1. 278 − 10 =
2. 838 − 10 =
3. 329 − 10 =
4. 757 − 10 =
5. 123 − 10 =
6. 993 − 10 =
7. 674 − 10 =
8. 524 − 10 =
9. 444 − 10 =
10. 242 − 10 =

GENERAL REVIEW 4

Solve each problem mentally.

1. $528 - 9 =$

2. $720 - 8 =$

3. $656 - 8 =$

4. $227 - 10 =$

5. $489 - 6 =$

6. $847 + 100 =$

7. $165 - 7 =$

8. $274 + 500 =$

9. $384 - 3 =$

10. $638 - 10 =$

Subtracting Two-Digit Numbers from Three-Digit Numbers (Part 1)

Strategy

$445 - 32$
$= (400 + 40 + 5) - (30 + 2)$ ❑ Expand the numbers into hundreds, tens, and ones.

$= (440 - 30) + (5 - 2)$ ❑ Arrange the numbers to subtract both the tens and ones values.

$= 410 + 3$ ❑ Add the numbers to find the answer.
$= \mathbf{413}$

Solve each problem mentally.

1. $647 - 23 =$

2. $286 - 71 =$

3. $334 - 12 =$

4. $862 - 52 =$

5. $429 - 13 =$

6. $798 - 44 =$

7. $552 - 31 =$

8. $943 - 22 =$

9. $188 - 47 =$

10. $256 - 24 =$

STRATEGY

Subtracting Two-Digit Numbers from Three-Digit Numbers (Part 2)

Strategy

$472 - 35 = (432 + 40) - 35$ ❑ Break up the three-digit number for easy subtraction.

$= 432 + (40 - 35)$ ❑ Subtract the two-digit numbers.

$= 432 + 5$ ❑ Add the numbers to find the answer.

$= \mathbf{437}$

Solve each problem mentally.

1. $743 - 38 =$

2. $132 - 26 =$

3. $369 - 57 =$

4. $422 - 14 =$

5. $281 - 35 =$

6. $551 - 49 =$

7. $895 - 78 =$

8. $973 - 62 =$

9. $654 - 34 =$

10. $596 - 83 =$

Subtracting Two-Digit Numbers from Three-Digit Numbers (Part 3)

Strategy

365 – 37 = 365 – (35 + 2)
- ❑ Break up the two-digit number for easy subtraction.

= (365 – 35) – 2
- ❑ Subtract the two-digit number from the three-digit number.

= 330 – 2
- ❑ Subtract the numbers to find the answer.

= **328**

Solve each problem mentally.

1. 243 – 28 =

2. 861 – 43 =

3. 334 – 26 =

4. 170 – 31 =

5. 594 – 76 =

6. 677 – 59 =

7. 485 – 68 =

8. 245 – 38 =

9. 983 – 37 =

10. 756 – 49 =

STRATEGY

Subtracting 99 from Three-Digit Numbers

Strategy

$551 - 99 = 551 - 100 + 1$
$= 451 + 1$
$= \mathbf{452}$

❑ Add 1 to 99 to make 100.
❑ Since 1 was added to 99, add 1 to find the answer.

Helpful Hint: The hundreds place in the answer decreases by 1 and the ones place in the answer increases by 1.

Solve each problem mentally.

1. $344 - 99 =$

2. $672 - 99 =$

3. $187 - 99 =$

4. $596 - 99 =$

5. $938 - 99 =$

6. $471 - 99 =$

7. $887 - 99 =$

8. $298 - 99 =$

9. $797 - 99 =$

10. $658 - 99 =$

Subtracting Two-Digit Numbers Ending with 9 from Three-Digit Numbers

Strategy

436 – 29

29 ≈ 30

436 – 29 = (436 – 30) + 1

= 406 + 1

= **407**

❑ Round the two-digit number up to the nearest ten.

❑ Subtract the numbers.

❑ Since 1 was added to 29 to make 30, add 1 to the difference to find the answer.

Solve each problem mentally.

1. 152 – 49 =

2. 893 – 89 =

3. 285 – 29 =

4. 688 – 79 =

5. 764 – 59 =

6. 922 – 69 =

7. 304 – 19 =

8. 531 – 39 =

9. 453 – 59 =

10. 623 – 79 =

GENERAL REVIEW 5

Solve each problem mentally.

1. 492 – 47 =

2. 625 – 13 =

3. 837 – 99 =

4. 268 – 51 =

5. 942 – 37 =

6. 581 – 78 =

7. 176 – 33 =

8. 731 – 25 =

9. 334 – 99 =

10. 548 – 29 =

STRATEGY

Subtracting Tens from Three-Digit Numbers

Strategy

$684 - 50 = (604 + 80) - 50$ ❑ Break up the three-digit number for easy subtraction.

$\quad\quad\quad = 604 + (80 - 50)$ ❑ Subtract the tens values.

$\quad\quad\quad = 604 + 30$ ❑ Add the numbers to find the answer.

$\quad\quad\quad = \mathbf{634}$

Solve each problem mentally.

1. $839 - 20 =$

2. $375 - 60 =$

3. $978 - 70 =$

4. $616 - 10 =$

5. $459 - 40 =$

6. $753 - 30 =$

7. $582 - 50 =$

8. $196 - 80 =$

9. $784 - 60 =$

10. $269 - 40 =$

STRATEGY

Subtracting 100 from Three-Digit Numbers

Strategy

843 − 100 = **743**

❑ Decrease the value in the hundreds place by 1.

Solve each problem mentally.

1. 296 − 100 =

2. 862 − 100 =

3. 546 − 100 =

4. 327 − 100 =

5. 189 − 100 =

6. 406 − 100 =

7. 794 − 100 =

8. 993 − 100 =

9. 354 − 100 =

10. 611 − 100 =

STRATEGY

Subtracting Three-Digit Numbers from Three-Digit Numbers (Part 1)

Strategy

356 − 213
= (300 + 50 + 6) − (200 + 10 + 3)

= (300 − 200) + (50 − 10) + (6 − 3)

= 100 + 40 + 3
= **143**

❑ Expand the numbers into hundreds, tens, and ones.

❑ Arrange the numbers to subtract the hundreds, tens, and ones values.

❑ Add the numbers to find the answer.

Solve each problem mentally.

1. 568 − 327 =

2. 873 − 431 =

3. 649 − 245 =

4. 335 − 124 =

5. 196 − 132 =

6. 947 − 637 =

7. 768 − 257 =

8. 487 − 356 =

9. 266 − 154 =

10. 779 − 538 =

Subtracting Three-Digit Numbers from Three-Digit Numbers (Part 2)

Strategy

$610 - 435 = (110 + 500) - 435$

$\quad\quad\quad\quad = 110 + (500 - 435)$
$\quad\quad\quad\quad = 110 + 65$
$\quad\quad\quad\quad = \textbf{175}$

❑ Break up the first three-digit number for easy subtraction.
❑ Subtract the numbers.
❑ Add the numbers to find the answer.

Solve each problem mentally.

1. $222 - 156 =$

2. $736 - 589 =$

3. $509 - 267 =$

4. $834 - 375 =$

5. $448 - 258 =$

6. $621 - 380 =$

7. $937 - 593 =$

8. $716 - 643 =$

9. $876 - 542 =$

10. $574 - 168 =$

STRATEGY

Subtracting Three-Digit Numbers from Three-Digit Numbers (Part 3)

Strategy

$985 - 437 = 985 - (435 + 2)$	❏ Break up the second three-digit number for easy subtraction.
$= (985 - 435) - 2$	❏ Subtract the three-digit numbers.
$= 550 - 2$	❏ Subtract the numbers to find the answer.
$= \mathbf{548}$	

Solve each problem mentally.

1. $367 - 229 =$

2. $863 - 426 =$

3. $656 - 338 =$

4. $953 - 717 =$

5. $248 - 109 =$

6. $546 - 238 =$

7. $762 - 459 =$

8. $472 - 126 =$

9. $951 - 538 =$

10. $674 - 217 =$

GENERAL REVIEW 6

Solve each problem mentally.

1. 683 – 100 =

2. 349 – 30 =

3. 765 – 232 =

4. 511 – 259 =

5. 436 – 158 =

6. 948 – 537 =

7. 896 – 60 =

8. 753 – 516 =

9. 281 – 137 =

10. 941 – 100 =

Subtracting Three-Digit Numbers Ending with 9 from Three-Digit Numbers

Strategy

756 – 349

349 ≈ 350

❏ Round the second three-digit number up to the nearest ten.

756 – 349 = (756 – 350) + 1
= 406 + 1
= **407**

❏ Subtract the numbers.

❏ Since 1 was added to 349 to make 350, add 1 to the difference to find the answer.

Solve each problem mentally.

1. 867 – 149 =

2. 971 – 659 =

3. 484 – 279 =

4. 572 – 359 =

5. 783 – 509 =

6. 695 – 489 =

7. 874 – 319 =

8. 396 – 189 =

9. 967 – 549 =

10. 782 – 469 =

STRATEGY

Subtracting Hundreds from Three-Digit Numbers

Strategy

$462 - 200 = $ **262**

❏ Subtract the hundreds values of both numbers.

Solve each problem mentally.

1. $925 - 600 =$

2. $506 - 300 =$

3. $983 - 800 =$

4. $754 - 500 =$

5. $868 - 700 =$

6. $793 - 600 =$

7. $347 - 200 =$

8. $678 - 400 =$

9. $842 - 700 =$

10. $711 - 500 =$

Multiplication: Using Repeated Addition

Strategy

$3 \times 4 = 4 + 4 + 4$

❑ When two numbers are multiplied, the answer can also be found with repeated addition. This problem shows 3 groups of 4.

$= 8 + 4$

$= \mathbf{12}$

❑ Add the numbers to find the answer.

Multiplication facts are widely used in mathematics. It is important to memorize the multiplication facts for 1 through 12.

Solve each problem mentally.

1. $4 \times 2 =$

2. $3 \times 3 =$

3. $2 \times 6 =$

4. $4 \times 5 =$

5. $2 \times 8 =$

6. $3 \times 6 =$

7. $2 \times 9 =$

8. $4 \times 9 =$

9. $2 \times 5 =$

10. $3 \times 7 =$

STRATEGY

Multiplying Numbers by 5

Strategy

$6 \times 5 = \textbf{30}$

$5 \times 5 = \textbf{25}$

❑ When even factors are multiplied by 5, the product will end in 0.

❑ When odd factors are multiplied by 5, the product will end in 5.

Factors × 5	Product Begins With
2 and 3	1
4 and 5	2
6 and 7	3
8 and 9	4

Solve each problem mentally.

1. $3 \times 5 =$

2. $9 \times 5 =$

3. $1 \times 5 =$

4. $7 \times 5 =$

5. $10 \times 5 =$

6. $8 \times 5 =$

7. $5 \times 5 =$

8. $2 \times 5 =$

9. $4 \times 5 =$

10. $6 \times 5 =$

WEEK 41

STRATEGY

Multiplying Numbers by 10

Strategy

12 × 10 = **120**

❑ To multiply numbers by 10, put a 0 after the factor.

Solve each problem mentally.

1. 10 × 10 =

2. 5 × 10 =

3. 8 × 10 =

4. 1 × 10 =

5. 6 × 10 =

6. 9 × 10 =

7. 7 × 10 =

8. 3 × 10 =

9. 2 × 10 =

10. 4 × 10 =

GENERAL REVIEW 7

Solve each problem mentally.

1. 431 – 128 =

2. 4 × 6 =

3. 3 × 5 =

4. 834 – 615 =

5. 9 × 5 =

6. 911 – 500 =

7. 4 × 5 =

8. 8 × 10 =

9. 548 – 300 =

10. 11 × 10 =

Dividing Numbers by 2, 3, and 4

Strategy

To divide numbers by 2, 3, and 4, use what you know about fact families. Division and multiplication are inverse operations.

$12 \div 2 = \mathbf{6}$ ☐ The related fact is $6 \times 2 = 12$.

Solve each problem mentally.

1. $24 \div 4 =$

2. $21 \div 3 =$

3. $12 \div 3 =$

4. $16 \div 4 =$

5. $14 \div 2 =$

6. $20 \div 2 =$

7. $15 \div 3 =$

8. $36 \div 4 =$

9. $27 \div 3 =$

10. $40 \div 4 =$

STRATEGY

Dividing Numbers by 5 and 10

Strategy

To divide numbers by 5, use what you know about the multiplication facts of 5.

$20 \div 5 = \textbf{4}$ ❑ The related fact is $4 \times 5 = 20$.

To divide numbers by 10, remove the 0 from the divisor.

$8\emptyset \div 10 = \textbf{8}$

Solve each problem mentally.

1. $30 \div 5 = $

2. $55 \div 5 = $

3. $30 \div 10 = $

4. $60 \div 10 = $

5. $40 \div 5 = $

6. $10 \div 10 = $

7. $15 \div 5 = $

8. $70 \div 10 = $

9. $25 \div 5 = $

10. $60 \div 5 = $

WEEK 45

GENERAL REVIEW 8

Solve each problem mentally.

1. $195 - 9 =$

2. $452 + 80 =$

3. $3 \times 10 =$

4. $607 + 99 =$

5. $916 - 48 =$

6. $734 + 100 =$

7. $18 \div 3 =$

8. $507 - 300 =$

9. $145 + 369 =$

10. $2 \times 8 =$

GENERAL REVIEW 9

Solve each problem mentally.

1. 158 + 85 =

2. 726 – 218 =

3. 361 + 72 =

4. 3 × 8 =

5. 506 – 8 =

6. 872 – 356 =

7. 426 + 10 =

8. 265 + 402 =

9. 45 ÷ 5 =

10. 618 – 100 =

GENERAL REVIEW 10

Solve each problem mentally.

1. $9 \times 10 =$

2. $12 \div 4 =$

3. $528 - 400 =$

4. $629 + 99 =$

5. $162 + 284 =$

6. $753 - 81 =$

7. $419 + 279 =$

8. $7 \times 5 =$

9. $367 + 90 =$

10. $24 \div 2 =$

GENERAL REVIEW 11

Solve each problem mentally.

1. $437 + 82 =$

2. $352 - 198 =$

3. $264 + 423 =$

4. $917 + 36 =$

5. $751 - 249 =$

6. $30 \div 5 =$

7. $8 \times 4 =$

8. $518 + 99 =$

9. $828 - 500 =$

10. $11 \times 10 =$

GENERAL REVIEW 12

Solve each problem mentally.

1. 567 – 80 =

2. 198 + 10 =

3. 837 – 318 =

4. 5 × 5 =

5. 863 + 9 =

6. 305 – 8 =

7. 2 × 4 =

8. 399 – 200 =

9. 463 + 507 =

10. 36 ÷ 3 =

GENERAL REVIEW 13

Solve each problem mentally.

1. 644 – 80 =

2. 289 + 199 =

3. 372 + 609 =

4. 3 × 7 =

5. 531 – 7 =

6. 749 + 55 =

7. 833 – 526 =

8. 90 ÷ 10 =

9. 498 – 100 =

10. 10 × 10 =

GENERAL REVIEW 14

Solve each problem mentally.

1. 505 + 89 =

2. 116 + 303 =

3. 860 − 259 =

4. 382 + 7 =

5. 278 + 700 =

6. 437 − 10 =

7. 5 × 9 =

8. 6 × 2 =

9. 55 ÷ 5 =

10. 728 + 16 =

GENERAL REVIEW 15

Solve each problem mentally.

1. 973 − 346 =

2. 110 ÷ 10 =

3. 572 + 80 =

4. 286 + 30 =

5. 6 × 5 =

6. 16 ÷ 4 =

7. 638 + 40 =

8. 349 − 82 =

9. 802 + 99 =

10. 369 + 179 =

Notes

WEEK 1		WEEK 2		WEEK 3		WEEK 4	
1.	277	1.	551	1.	792	1.	398
2.	193	2.	942	2.	151	2.	980
3.	459	3.	301	3.	611	3.	284
4.	768	4.	192	4.	943	4.	695
5.	289	5.	442	5.	333	5.	820
6.	839	6.	561	6.	452	6.	436
7.	727	7.	383	7.	912	7.	153
8.	329	8.	664	8.	282	8.	768
9.	189	9.	752	9.	833	9.	513
10.	866	10.	842	10.	524	10.	857

WEEK 5		WEEK 6		WEEK 7		WEEK 8	
1.	861	1.	824	1.	751	1.	586
2.	181	2.	626	2.	196	2.	203
3.	430	3.	824	3.	552	3.	675
4.	573	4.	739	4.	974	4.	523
5.	251	5.	265	5.	370	5.	262
6.	483	6.	116	6.	497	6.	423
7.	693	7.	987	7.	889	7.	962
8.	772	8.	456	8.	692	8.	835
9.	870	9.	382	9.	301	9.	926
10.	403	10.	554	10.	600	10.	202

WEEK 9		WEEK 10		WEEK 11		WEEK 12	
1.	375	1.	268	1.	292	1.	597
2.	751	2.	928	2.	873	2.	961
3.	567	3.	548	3.	566	3.	352
4.	912	4.	778	4.	476	4.	468
5.	490	5.	178	5.	477	5.	862
6.	647	6.	738	6.	693	6.	693
7.	232	7.	908	7.	891	7.	508
8.	965	8.	628	8.	778	8.	781
9.	828	9.	398	9.	398	9.	226
10.	486	10.	678	10.	175	10.	982

WEEK 13		WEEK 14		WEEK 15		WEEK 16	
1.	469	1.	460	1.	429	1.	645
2.	736	2.	840	2.	887	2.	892
3.	952	3.	740	3.	897	3.	983
4.	275	4.	970	4.	758	4.	717
5.	351	5.	650	5.	947	5.	953
6.	752	6.	660	6.	689	6.	777
7.	549	7.	930	7.	779	7.	951
8.	648	8.	850	8.	988	8.	983
9.	993	9.	840	9.	717	9.	905
10.	817	10.	950	10.	598	10.	734

WEEK 17

1. 788
2. 848
3. 898
4. 688
5. 878
6. 928
7. 568
8. 608
9. 898
10. 688

WEEK 18

1. 876
2. 420
3. 669
4. 960
5. 968
6. 788
7. 748
8. 738
9. 479
10. 980

WEEK 19

1. 793
2. 982
3. 855
4. 903
5. 775
6. 843
7. 991
8. 568
9. 847
10. 990

WEEK 20

1. 383
2. 753
3. 580
4. 421
5. 813
6. 230
7. 691
8. 191
9. 911
10. 441

WEEK 21

1. 266
2. 729
3. 927
4. 154
5. 377
6. 398
7. 557
8. 607
9. 828
10. 369

WEEK 22

1. 316
2. 648
3. 187
4. 288
5. 752
6. 589
7. 405
8. 809
9. 357
10. 706

WEEK 23

1. 268
2. 828
3. 319
4. 747
5. 113
6. 983
7. 664
8. 514
9. 434
10. 232

WEEK 24

1. 519
2. 712
3. 648
4. 217
5. 483
6. 947
7. 158
8. 774
9. 381
10. 628

WEEK 25

1. 624
2. 215
3. 322
4. 810
5. 416
6. 754
7. 521
8. 921
9. 141
10. 232

WEEK 26

1. 705
2. 106
3. 312
4. 408
5. 246
6. 502
7. 817
8. 911
9. 620
10. 513

WEEK 27

1. 215
2. 818
3. 308
4. 139
5. 518
6. 618
7. 417
8. 207
9. 946
10. 707

WEEK 28

1. 245
2. 573
3. 88
4. 497
5. 839
6. 372
7. 788
8. 199
9. 698
10. 559

WEEK 29

1. 103
2. 804
3. 256
4. 609
5. 705
6. 853
7. 285
8. 492
9. 394
10. 544

WEEK 30

1. 445
2. 612
3. 738
4. 217
5. 905
6. 503
7. 143
8. 706
9. 235
10. 519

WEEK 31

1. 819
2. 315
3. 908
4. 606
5. 419
6. 723
7. 532
8. 116
9. 724
10. 229

WEEK 32

1. 196
2. 762
3. 446
4. 227
5. 89
6. 306
7. 694
8. 893
9. 254
10. 511

WEEK 33		WEEK 34		WEEK 35		WEEK 36	
1.	241	1.	66	1.	138	1.	583
2.	442	2.	147	2.	437	2.	319
3.	404	3.	242	3.	318	3.	533
4.	211	4.	459	4.	236	4.	252
5.	64	5.	190	5.	139	5.	278
6.	310	6.	241	6.	308	6.	411
7.	511	7.	344	7.	303	7.	836
8.	131	8.	73	8.	346	8.	237
9.	112	9.	334	9.	413	9.	144
10.	241	10.	406	10.	457	10.	841

WEEK 37		WEEK 38		WEEK 39		WEEK 40	
1.	718	1.	325	1.	8	1.	15
2.	312	2.	206	2.	9	2.	45
3.	205	3.	183	3.	12	3.	5
4.	213	4.	254	4.	20	4.	35
5.	274	5.	168	5.	16	5.	50
6.	206	6.	193	6.	18	6.	40
7.	555	7.	147	7.	18	7.	25
8.	207	8.	278	8.	36	8.	10
9.	418	9.	142	9.	10	9.	20
10.	313	10.	211	10.	21	10.	30

WEEK 41		WEEK 42		WEEK 43		WEEK 44	
1.	100	1.	303	1.	6	1.	6
2.	50	2.	24	2.	7	2.	11
3.	80	3.	15	3.	4	3.	3
4.	10	4.	219	4.	4	4.	6
5.	60	5.	45	5.	7	5.	8
6.	90	6.	411	6.	10	6.	1
7.	70	7.	20	7.	5	7.	3
8.	30	8.	80	8.	9	8.	7
9.	20	9.	248	9.	9	9.	5
10.	40	10.	110	10.	10	10.	12

WEEK 45		WEEK 46		WEEK 47		WEEK 48	
1.	186	1.	243	1.	90	1.	519
2.	532	2.	508	2.	3	2.	154
3.	30	3.	433	3.	128	3.	687
4.	706	4.	24	4.	728	4.	953
5.	868	5.	498	5.	446	5.	502
6.	834	6.	516	6.	672	6.	6
7.	6	7.	436	7.	698	7.	32
8.	207	8.	667	8.	35	8.	617
9.	514	9.	9	9.	457	9.	328
10.	16	10.	518	10.	12	10.	110

WEEK *49*	WEEK *50*	WEEK *51*	WEEK *52*
1. 487	**1.** 564	**1.** 594	**1.** 627
2. 208	**2.** 488	**2.** 419	**2.** 11
3. 519	**3.** 981	**3.** 601	**3.** 652
4. 25	**4.** 21	**4.** 389	**4.** 316
5. 872	**5.** 524	**5.** 978	**5.** 30
6. 297	**6.** 804	**6.** 427	**6.** 4
7. 8	**7.** 307	**7.** 45	**7.** 678
8. 199	**8.** 9	**8.** 12	**8.** 267
9. 970	**9.** 398	**9.** 11	**9.** 901
10. 12	**10.** 100	**10.** 744	**10.** 548